Advent: The Season of Surp

Except where noted, all Scriptures are taken from the Christian Standard Bible (CSB)

Editor: Sandie Siemons, Dorothy Littell Greco

ISBN 979-8-86544-226-4

www.YvonneVSanchez.com

ADVENT

THE SEASON OF SURPRISE

YVONNE V. SÁNCHEZ

TABLE OF CONTENTS

ACKNOWLEDGMENTS

I will always be grateful to Andrea Moore for leading me through the Exchange for the first time. This practice gave me the opportunity to lay down my burdens regularly and my life is consistently lighter, because of it. This process has made the Scripture, "My burden is easy and my yoke is light" (John 10:10), a reality in my life.

I want to thank Sandie Siemons for the gift of her work. Special thanks to Cindy Taylor, whose encouragement, redirection, and thought-provoking questions helped me discover my identity as an author. Tara Richards for her patient technical support. I'd like to give an immense *thank you* to my husband, Armando. Through everyday conversations, he helped me discover my target audience.

INTRODUCTION

The Bible is full of surprises. No matter how often I read a chapter, a story, or a verse, I discover new things. I heard the Christmas story over and over as a child and loved it. When I became a Christian, the story came alive. I was awed by God's perfect plan. He surprised Mary, a naive teen who said "yes" to an angel, God's messenger. God chose Joseph, a carpenter, to be Jesus's adoptive father. His qualifications were a humble and obedient heart. Jesus was born in a stable instead of a palace. He stooped down from his throne to be born just like the people he would die for. The surprises go on and on.

I want you to enjoy the Christmas season with a deeper understanding of God's plan for humankind and your life. As you start the new year, I pray you will be more confident of how he chose you and needs you to expand his Kingdom. In this Advent season, let yourself be awed by new aspects of his Word and connect them to your life and calling.

HOW TO USE THIS BOOK

There are twenty-four chapters in the book of Luke, and a devotional for each chapter. You can read one devotional daily, beginning December 1st. I challenge you to read the entire chapter of Scripture before engaging with the daily text. I will share a surprise I discovered in each chapter. It might be connected to the characters in the story, a personal revelation, or the result of research.

Each day ends with reflective questions. Question two will always direct you to pray or journal.

PRAYER

Prayer is talking to God. It doesn't have to be formal or take place in a particular location. You might talk to God while you take a walk, drive, or load the dishwasher. When you talk to God, you should also listen for a response. He might respond with a Bible verse or a thought might come to your mind that you did not initiate. Talking and listening are two important elements of a rich prayer life.

JOURNALING

Journaling is another way to sort through your thoughts and communicate with God. I have included blank pages at the end of the book for this purpose. I use words and images when I journal. I might begin with a question, a Bible verse, or my own feelings. I invite Holy Spirit to be with me because I want to hear from the Lord. Oftentimes, God gives me an image that supports the ideas on the page. Although I'm not an artist, I do my best to capture that image. When I'm finished, I have clarity and direction. As I proceed with my day, the words and images come back to me and keep me focused on God's will.

GO DEEPER

The questions are created to provoke thought and to help you self-reflect. Some questions might agitate something in your soul that needs attention or that weighs you down. If you need to work through a delicate issue, you can use a tool I have included in Appendix 1. *The Exchange* is a process I regularly use to keep my soul healthy. You will develop a more intimate relationship with God as you use it.

Enjoy your journey in the life of Jesus and expect to be surprised!

Yvonne

FOREWORD

It is with great joy and enthusiasm that I write this foreword for my dear friend Yvonne V. Sánchez and her new Advent devotional, *Advent: The Season of Surprise*. I have had the privilege of walking closely with Yvonne for many years, and I have witnessed firsthand the sincerity of her faith and her unwavering commitment to Christ.

Yvonne is not only a trusted coach and mentor in my own life, but she has also been a remarkable leader within our church community. Her ability to communicate God's Word in a way that is both clear and actionable for every day is truly a gift. Yvonne has a genuine passion to see believers succeed in every area of their lives and has dedicated herself to walking alongside others as a coach and mentor.

In this devotional, Yvonne invites you on a transformative journey through the Advent season. As you read each chapter, you will encounter the surprises found within the pages of Scripture. The Christmas story, which may have become familiar to us over the years, comes alive with new depth and meaning as Yvonne explores the unexpected twists and turns of God's perfect plan.

I encourage you to set aside a quiet and sacred space each day leading up to Christmas to engage with this devotional. Yvonne's insights and reflections will deepen your understanding of God's plan for humanity and your own personal journey. As we enter the new year, my prayer is that you will grow in confidence, knowing that you are chosen by God and uniquely equipped to expand His Kingdom.

Each chapter of this devotional is thoughtfully crafted, drawing from the 24 chapters of the book of Luke. Yvonne masterfully shares a surprise she has discovered in each chapter, whether it be a revelation from the characters in the story or a personal insight she has gained. Allow yourself to be awed by new aspects of God's Word and make meaningful connections to your own life and calling.

To fully immerse yourself in this devotional experience, I encourage you to read the entire chapter before engaging with Yvonne's reflections. By doing so, you will prime your heart and mind, allowing the devotional to deepen your understanding and enhance your spiritual growth. Yvonne has also included reflective questions at the end of each entry, guiding you to further explore the truths revealed.

As an added resource, Yvonne has thoughtfully provided Appendix I, which includes "The Exchange" tool. This powerful tool will help you exchange your burdens for God's blessings, fostering a healthier and more intimate relationship with Him.

I am confident that as you embark on this Advent journey with Yvonne, you will be surprised, inspired, and transformed. May this devotional draw you closer to the heart of Christ and ignite a renewed sense of awe and wonder in your faith. May you experience the joy of the season and anticipate the beautiful surprises that await you.

Sincerely,
Stephen Martin
Senior Pastor, Vintage Church, Founder of Church Sherpa
& President of Church Leadership College

DAY 1: IN THE BEGINNING

READ LUKE, CHAPTER 1

"Then the angel told her, 'Do not be afraid, Mary, for you have found favor with God. Now listen: You will conceive and give birth to a son, and you will name Him Jesus. He will be great and will be called the Son of the Most High, and the Lord God will give Him the throne of his father, David. He will reign over the house of Jacob forever, and his Kingdom will have no end.'"

Luke 1:30-33

From the moment Adam and Eve fell into sin, humankind was separated from God. There are seventy-seven generations between Adam and Jesus. Israel was in a waiting pattern for thousands of years. God broke in when the angel Gabriel surprised Mary, an unwed teenager, and delivered the news that God had chosen her to be the mother of the Savior. Mary surprised Joseph with news of the pregnancy, and Joseph surprisingly married her.

A WELCOME SURPRISE

Did you know Elohim, the Creator, spoke about Jesus in Genesis 3 when Adam and Eve fell into sin? According to Scripture, God told the serpent, "I will put hostility between you and the woman and between your offspring and her offspring. He will strike your head, and you will strike his heel." (Genesis 3:15).

God's perfect plan for our redemption began with a situation that appeared sinful and chaotic. Mary and Joseph couldn't control the narrative. They surrendered to a plan they had no power over, and God made sense of the chaos.

We all have occurrences in our lives we didn't look for— happenings that don't seem to align with a Spirit-led life. We can imitate Mary and

Joseph by aligning ourselves with God's will through surrender amid chaos and confusion. We can stop demanding to understand and choose to let God have control.

1. What events or circumstances have surprised you or felt chaotic, uncontrollable, and maybe even ungodly?

2. Pray or journal about surrendering this situation.

DAY 2: SECRETS REVEALED

READ LUKE, CHAPTER 2

"Now, Master, you can dismiss your servant in peace, as you promised. For my eyes have seen your salvation. You have prepared it in the presence of all peoples—a light for revelation to the Gentiles and glory to your people Israel."

Luke 2:29-32

The infant Jesus was taken to the temple in Jerusalem at the age of six weeks. He was dedicated, in compliance with the Law and Jewish practice. Simeon was an older, devout man in the community, and he was moved by the Spirit to enter the temple at the very time Mary and Joseph were there.

A WELCOME SURPRISE

In Hebrew, Simeon means hearing or listening. God promised Simeon that he would see the Messiah. Who knows how long he had waited or what he thought the Messiah would look like? There might have been dozens of young couples dedicating their children on the same day Simeon went to the temple. He knew the voice of God. When he looked past an ordinary-looking couple, he recognized the Savior of the world. He realized God would fulfill the promise of salvation through this six-week-old boy. Simeon acted on the revelation, lifted the child, and declared the infant to be the Messiah.

We can each witness things hidden from sight when we develop sensitivity to God's voice, like Simeon did. When we clear our minds and give him attention, we create a God filter. The God filter allows us to see and be a part of things others miss.

1. Can you name a time when your mind and heart were open and focused on Him, and you experienced something others likely missed?

2. Pray or journal about your God filter. If you've not experienced this, ask God to open your eyes to see what has been hidden.

DAY 3: 183° TURN

READ LUKE, CHAPTER 3

"Therefore, produce fruit consistent with repentance. And don't start saying to yourselves, 'We have Abraham as our father,' for I tell you that God is able to raise up children for Abraham from these stones. The ax is already at the root of the trees. Therefore, every tree that doesn't produce good fruit will be cut down and thrown into the fire."

Luke 3:8-9

There is a thirty-year difference between Chapter 2 and Chapter 3. John the Baptist and Jesus are grown men in Chapter 3. The Israelites focused on obedience for hundreds of years when John, an animated preacher, surprised Israel with a new message—the message of repentance. He preached this message to everyone and made it clear that NO ONE is good; everyone must turn away from their selfish life and turn to God. John preached a new message and he preached it with fire. Surprisingly, the fiery message affected people's hearts. John's message even affected the tax collectors who cooperated with the Roman empire to overtax Jewish brethren.

A WELCOME SURPRISE

Tax collectors were callous. They took advantage of their Jewish brothers. Their callous hearts were affected by John's message. They were baptized and asked John, "What shall we do?" [to change our lives].

John made it clear that a repentant life bears good fruit. A repentant life gives generously, doesn't steal from others, doesn't abuse anyone, or complain about what they don't have. Repentance is a heart issue, but it didn't make obedience obsolete. John obeyed God's assignment when he surprised Israel and told them to change the focus of their lives.

Repentance is not a one-time occurrence; it's a way of life. To bear the fruit John spoke of, we must practice confession, forgiveness, and repentance. In verses 19 and 20, John rebuked Herod because he was an adulterer. Herod refused to repent, and he sent John to prison. We are all capable of being stubborn and prideful like Herod. Without regularly admitting our shortcomings, we'll do what he did, lock people out of our lives and hold on to our wickedness.

1. What areas of your life are stubborn and prideful?

2. Pray or journal and ask God to reveal to you where the stubbornness and pride come from. Are they family traits? Can you track them to an event that made you begin to protect yourself? Do you resist correction?

DAY 4: SENT

READ LUKE, CHAPTER 4

"The Spirit of the Lord is on me because he has anointed me to preach good news to the poor. He has sent me to proclaim release to the captives and recovery of sight to the blind, to set free the oppressed, to proclaim the year of the Lord's favor."

Luke 4:18-19

Jesus was born in Bethlehem and raised in Nazareth, in the southern part of Israel. He began his formal ministry in Galilee, a province in northern Israel. He taught in the synagogues, and the people recognized the wisdom and depth of his teaching. They received him, and he gained fame in Galilee. Afterward, he went to Nazareth and went to the synagogue to teach. The people's response was the exact opposite of those in Galilee. The Scripture says, "Everyone in the synagogue was enraged. They got up, drove him out of town, and brought him to the edge of the hill their town was built on, intending to hurl him over the cliff. But he passed right through the crowd and went on his way" (Luke 4:28-30).

He returned to Galilee, and again, he was loved, respected, and received. He performed miracles there such as healing the sick and casting out demons. Scripture says, "It is necessary for me to proclaim the good news about the Kingdom of God to the other towns also, because I was sent for this purpose" (Luke 4:43).

A WELCOME SURPRISE

Jesus went many places, but his mission to release the captive, restore sight to the blind, and free those who were oppressed only came true in the places where he was received and hearts were open.

When he spoke the words of Isaiah about himself, everyone within hearing distance was startled. Did anyone expect to hear him say he was the Messiah? Some believed and some didn't. Miracles were abundant where people were open to his encouragement, teaching, and correction. He changed their lives. He infused them with hope, and the people that rejected him remained the same. Darkness and hopelessness persisted in their homes and communities. Light and joy were available by choice.

1. Are there certain areas of your life where you find it easy to believe in God's promises and others where you struggle to believe? If so, how do you explain the difference?

2. Pray or journal about areas of your life where doubt might be impeding the miraculous.

DAY 5: LET GO!

READ CHAPTER 5

"Then everyone was astounded, and they were giving glory to God."

Luke 5:26

These words describe the reaction when Jesus healed a paralyzed man in Galilee. Healing people and casting out demons caused some people to follow him and others to be suspicious of him.

Luke tells us Jesus went out and saw a tax collector named Levi sitting at his tax booth. When Jesus said, "Follow me," Levi got up, left everything, and followed him (Luke 5:27-28). Tax collectors were a despised group of people. These Jewish men collected exorbitant taxes for the Roman government and added fees for themselves. The Pharisees hated tax collectors because of their association with the Roman Empire. Jesus spent time eating and fellowshipping with them, which is one reason the Pharisees built a case against him. In their minds, good Jewish citizens did not associate with tax collectors. When they asked him about the company he kept, Jesus responded, "It is not the healthy who need a doctor, but the sick. I have not come to call the righteous, but sinners to repentance" (Luke 5:31-32).

What was the difference between people who were astounded and gave glory to God, and the Pharisees who used the same events to build a case against Jesus? I think it's safe to say the Pharisees felt threatened. They cared more about rules and external appearances than whether their hearts were being changed. Furthermore they expected others to conform to their beliefs.

A WELCOME SURPRISE

Even followers of Christ struggle with the desire to control. We put up walls to defend our thinking and behavior.

Although we are new creations in Christ, we will always be tempted to control our surroundings, and expect others to act, speak, or think like us. When Jesus went into the wilderness, Satan tempted him to take control of his own life and exercise his power rather than surrender to the Father's plan (Matthew 4:1-11). He overcame temptation with prayer and Scripture. The Holy Spirit will always lead and guide us away from directing our own lives and toward following God and his plan.

1. Which areas of life do you feel pressured to control instead of trusting God?

2. Pray or journal and talk to God about what triggers your fear when you aren't in control.

DAY 6: LOOK IN THE MIRROR

READ CHAPTER 6

"Then Jesus said to them, 'I ask you: Is it lawful to do good on the Sabbath or to do evil, to save life or to destroy it?' After looking around at them all, he told him, 'Stretch out your hand.' He did, and his hand was restored."

Luke 6:9-10

This healing took place in the synagogue on the Sabbath, a day designated for rest. This and other actions caused the Pharisees to see Jesus as an enemy of the Law because he disrupted Israel's traditions. Jesus didn't oppose the Law or promote disobedience but he did encourage his followers to think about obedience in a new way. He moved them through parables and stories. He taught them to forgive and love their enemies. They obeyed because they loved him.

The Jewish people expected their Messiah to be a warrior like King David. They believed he would go to battle and deliver them from their enemies. But Jesus delivered the truth that when we lack humility and repentance, we are God's enemies.

A WELCOME SURPRISE

The only way to love your enemy as yourself is through the humble recognition that we are the enemy, outside of the forgiveness God offers each of us.

Jesus's mission pushed against the grain of the culture and societal practices and expectations. He didn't come with a physical sword to raise up an army that would defeat the Romans. Instead, his words served as a sword that cut through inaccurate beliefs to access the heart, and the army he mobilized would conquer people and nations with mercy and truth.

Will you fight for God's Kingdom by growing in humility, relying on God's truth, and resisting the pressures of our culture?

1. What practices and beliefs compel you to fight for your own rights instead of for God's Kingdom?

2. Pray or journal about your struggle to protect and defend yourself.

DAY 7: RADICAL FAITH

READ CHAPTER 7

"Lord, don't trouble yourself, since I am not worthy to have you come under my roof. That is why I didn't even consider myself worthy to come to you. But say the word, and my servant will be healed."

Luke 7:6b-7

A Roman centurion's slave was on his deathbed. News of Jesus's ministry reached the centurion's ears, and he sent Jewish leaders to request that Jesus save his slave's life. Jesus's actions must have stupefied many. He was as responsive to a Roman soldier's need as he was to the needs of his Jewish brothers and sisters.

Romans worshiped Roman gods. With so many gods to choose from in his own culture, the centurion put his faith in this Rabbi, who had been gaining notoriety across Israel and Judea. Jesus didn't interrogate the centurion about what god he worshiped. He didn't discuss the oppressive Roman occupation. He just met his need. Jesus responded to the soldier's request and as he headed to the centurion's home, the soldier stopped him with the statement, "I'm not worthy that you should enter my home, but say a word, and my servant would be healed."

Somehow, Jesus activated the centurion's faith. He had complete confidence that Jesus's words had the power to heal. The man's faith amazed Jesus and he declared the centurion's faith greater than anyone in all of Israel. Jesus saw past the man's ethnicity, occupation, and politics. He responded to the man's heart.

If your child was sick, would you say to the doctor, "Just pronounce that my child is well, and I'm sure it will be so"? The soldier recognized Jesus's power and authority.

A WELCOME SURPRISE

The centurion demonstrated what it looks like to have radical faith in Christ's power to heal—even if Jesus is not physically present.

The centurion's actions inspire us to put our faith in him when we are in need. This imperfect and sinful Roman soldier summoned the courage to approach Jesus. He was subject to consequences if the Roman authorities discovered he sought Jesus out, but he humbled himself and called Jesus, Lord.

1. Where does your faith reflect the centurion's strong and stable faith?

2. Pray or journal about areas of your life where you struggle with doubt.

DAY 8: FAITH IN THE STORM

READ CHAPTER 8

"Then he got up and rebuked the wind and the raging waves. So they ceased, and there was a calm. He said to them, 'Where is your faith?'"

Luke 8:24b-25

Jesus and His disciples were crossing the lake in a boat. A fierce storm hit as Jesus slept. He calmed the storm after they woke him crying, "Master, Master, we're going to die." Several disciples were fishermen and well acquainted with life on the water. They had witnessed healings and deliverances. They believed he had the authority to forgive sin. They were with him when he rocked cultural norms. Each man had his own story about why he chose to follow Jesus. So why did they panic in this situation? Their fears caused them to doubt his sovereignty. Jesus mirrored this back to them and essentially asked, "How did this storm steal your confidence?"

The disciples' faith was growing. They were certain Jesus could heal bodies and perceive the unseen but the storm shook them and fear overcame their faith.

A WELCOME SURPRISE

When Jesus awoke, he strategically gave them what they needed to regain their faith; he ordered the storm to stop. He worked a miracle to help them reset before asking, "Where is your faith?"

If I had been in the boat, the question would have made me ask, "If I'm sure about his identity, should the storm have made me tremble?" When we exercise faith, we grow. Raging winds and rough waters reveal our doubts and test our faith. We need storms to strengthen our beliefs about who God is and the place he has in our lives.

1. Talk about a storm you've experienced and how you responded to that storm. How did your faith impact your response?

2. Pray or journal about your faith. Is it growing or stagnant?

DAY 9: CALCULATE THE COST

READ CHAPTER 9

"Summoning the Twelve, he gave them power and authority over all the demons and to heal diseases. Then he sent them to proclaim the Kingdom of God and to heal the sick."

Luke 9:1

This chapter describes the apostles' internship. In chapter six, Jesus chose the twelve, and in this chapter, he gave them power and authority to replicate the miracles he performed. Jesus was more than a gifted teacher. He was the Savior, and the disciples watched him make broken people whole. Can you imagine the zeal that drove them to do what they had seen him do? They witnessed spiritual, physical, emotional, and mental transformations every day.

In the midst of their excitement, did any of the disciples second-guess their commitment? Were they aware of the price they would pay to be his disciple?

A WELCOME SURPRISE

These zealous young men committed themselves to Jesus's message. He explained some would pay a high price to follow him. They were unaware that most of them would give their lives for the gospel.

Anyone who has surrendered to Christ will pay a price. There is a minimal chance you or I will lose our lives for the gospel. However, by standing up for the Gospel, we might be ridiculed, abandoned, or experience financial loss. What price are you willing to pay to be a disciple of Christ?

1. Where is it easy for you to share the Gospel? Where is it difficult and what makes it difficult?

2. Pray or journal about areas where you lack boldness.

DAY 10: YOU CAN DO IT TOO!

READ CHAPTER 10

"Look, I have given you the authority to trample on snakes and scorpions and over all the power of the enemy; nothing at all will harm you. However, don't rejoice that the spirits submit to you, but rejoice that your names are written in heaven."

Luke 10:19-20

The book of Luke reads like a novel to me. I see the primary character, Jesus, with secondary characters that either support him (apostles and faithful followers) or work against him (Pharisees and Roman officials). I see the rising action and am beginning to feel dread about the climax. Throughout this chapter, the author continues the theme of multiplication and reveals the role of Jesus's followers in affecting change in the world.

In this section, Jesus sent seventy more followers to share his message. Once again, he gave them specific instructions. When they returned, they reported their experiences with astonishment, saying, "Lord, even the demons submit to us in your name" (Luke 10:17).

A WELCOME SURPRISE

They were no longer just his students. They were performing miracles too!

Jesus responded to them with sobering words. He reminded them that he had equipped them with power and authority, and that it wasn't about them.

Christians should affect change without drawing attention to ourselves. The presence of God within us allows us to point to Jesus. The peace and power we carry can speak to other's uncertainties and questions, such as, "Is this all there is?" We should never underestimate the power of Christ within us.

1. In what ways are you aware of God's presence in and around you?

2. Pray or journal and ask God to help you identify things that block your awareness of his presence.

DAY 11: PRAY LIKE JESUS

READ CHAPTER 11

"One day Jesus was praying in a certain place. When he finished, one of his disciples said to him, 'Lord, teach us to pray, just as John taught his disciples.'"

Luke 11:1

The disciple asked for a lesson in prayer. He saw something in Jesus's prayer time that he wanted. Like a good teacher, Jesus responded to the request. The following few verses are what we have come to know as *The Lord's Prayer*. As a child, I memorized this as a part of my Roman Catholic catechism. My sister Norma and I shared a bedroom. In elementary school, we had twin beds with yellow chenille bedspreads. Every night at bedtime, the two of us and our mom knelt by our beds and recited the Lord's Prayer. I am grateful our parents showed us how to end the day with honor and respect for God.

A WELCOME SURPRISE

The Lord's Prayer teaches us to pray like Jesus prayed.

As an adult, I learned to use this prayer as a template. Here's a condensed version of that teaching:

Our Father who art in Heaven, hallowed be thy name. Begin all prayer by recognizing who you are praying to.

Thy Kingdom come, thy will be done, on Earth as it is in Heaven. Jesus taught us that the focus of prayer is God's will, not self-will.

Give us this day our daily bread. This statement recognizes God as the source of all we have and need.

Forgive us this day as we forgive our trespassers. Confession, forgiveness, and repentance should be a part of our daily lives.

Lead us not into temptation but deliver us from evil. We all face temptation and need Jesus's resurrection power to resist it. The Holy Spirit guides, supports, and empowers us.

During Advent, we prepare to celebrate the anniversary of his birth and prepare for his second coming. Prayer changes us. Whether you pray the Lord's Prayer verbatim or as a pattern, the words and the meaning behind them can transform us into Spirit-led, Kingdom-focused disciples.

1. What can you do to pray more effectively?

2. Pray or journal about people God wants you to pray for.

DAY 12: LOVE AND TRUTH

READ CHAPTER 12

"I tell you, my friends, do not be afraid of those who kill the body and after that can do no more. But I will show you whom you should fear: Fear Him who, after your body has been killed, has authority to throw you into hell. Yes, I tell you, fear him."

Luke 12:4-5

In this chapter, Jesus's teachings are directed to his followers. The language is strong and the topic is judgment. He was clear about the risk of following him. Human judgment brings shame that only lasts for our time on earth, but God's judgment lasts forever. The purpose of these words was to keep his followers focused on eternity.

In the following sentence, Jesus softens the tone. "Aren't five sparrows sold for two pennies? Yet not one of them is forgotten in God's sight. Indeed, the hairs of your head are all counted. Don't be afraid; you are worth more than many sparrows." (Luke 12:6-7).

He used the story of the sparrows to show how important each person was to him, and to prepare the disciples for persecution. They would feel lonely and forgotten in their time of persecution. They could hold on to an image of his attention to insignificant sparrows during rough times.

A WELCOME SURPRISE

God embodies both love and truth. He loves us perfectly and individually. That love changes us and makes us willing to give up everything for his sake.

Jesus's communication was strategic. He made each person feel seen and valued. The first martyrs would need to hold on to this truth in the midst of being persecuted.

God is omnipotent. He can build up or tear down at will. He can pour out abundant blessings or take everything away. His followers can be confident that God will never forget them.

1. What price have you paid to follow Christ?

2. Pray or journal about the sufferings and hardships Christians across the globe face today.

DAY 13: THERE'S PEACE IN PURPOSE

READ CHAPTER 13

"At that time, some Pharisees came and told him, 'Go, get out of here. Herod wants to kill you.' He said to them, 'Go tell that fox, "Look, I'm driving out demons and performing healings today and tomorrow, and on the third day I will complete my work." Yet it is necessary that I travel today, tomorrow, and the next day, because it is not possible for a prophet to perish outside of Jerusalem.'"

Luke 13:31-33

Herod's threat would not deter him from his mission. You and I are the focus of that mission. Jesus was referring to himself when he said, "No prophet can die outside of Jerusalem." He knew how it would all end—with his death on the cross—but he wouldn't be distracted from completing his mission. The Pharisee warned him of something he was already preparing for.

A WELCOME SURPRISE

Herod's threat shook the Pharisees but had no effect on Jesus. The Pharisees were unaware of Jesus's purpose on Earth and therefore acted as if human intervention would help Jesus.

The following verses express Jesus's grief about Jerusalem and her people.

"Jerusalem, Jerusalem, who kills the prophets and stones those who are sent to her. How often I wanted

to gather your children together, as a hen gathers her chicks under her wings, but you were not willing."
Luke 13:34-35

In these verses, Jesus lamented over the city that would forget the miracles and extraordinary teachings. Jerusalem was the city that would demand his death. The people he ate with, loved, and served would turn against him so that he could complete the mission he and his Father agreed on. The Son would sacrifice himself so that every human could have everlasting life.

Threats have an impact when we are unaware of our purpose. They mean nothing when a personal mission is clearly established.

1. During the Christmas season, Satan seems particularly active. He wants God's people to worry instead of celebrate. He heightens stress in relationships. He manipulates career problems or attacks with illness. How is he trying to keep you from focusing on the celebration of Christmas?

2. Pray or journal about how to remain focused on the most important things during this Christmas season.

DAY 14: LIFE IS A BANQUET

READ CHAPTER 14

"When you give a luncheon or dinner, do not invite your friends, your brothers or sisters, your relatives, or your rich neighbors; if you do, they may invite you back and so you will be repaid. But when you give a banquet, invite the poor, the crippled, the lame, the blind, and you will be blessed. Although they cannot repay you, you will be repaid at the resurrection of the righteous."

Luke 14:12-14

Jesus was the greatest teacher who ever lived. His teachings invited people to examine their lives, motivations, and thoughts. His followers saw him live out his teachings. He demonstrated how he wants us to live.

It is easy to read these verses and assume we should donate to the food pantry or coat drive and support groups that provide disaster relief. Such actions help, but Jesus is asking us to give sacrificially. This section of Scripture makes it clear that there is a blessing when we give sacrificially to those who are less fortunate.

A WELCOME SURPRISE

When Jesus is Lord, our entire life is a banquet.

We are challenged to imitate his life. Your teacher expects you to reflect and put his words into action. Who do you invite to the banqueting table? Do you invite lonely people for dinner? Do you befriend someone who doesn't have friends? Is there someone you don't really care for and God wants you to hear their story?

1. Sacrificial giving is uncomfortable. If you never feel discomfort, you may be playing it too safe. When was the last time you felt discomfort because of sacrificial giving?

2. Pray or journal about who God might want you to invite to your banquet table.

DAY 15: THREE STORIES

READ CHAPTER 15

"This man welcomes sinners and eats with them."

Luke 15:2

I want to share a little about Luke, the author of this book. He was not an eyewitness to the life of Jesus or one of the original twelve apostles. He was a physician, and his writings made him an early historian for the Church. He became a follower soon after Jesus's resurrection. The book of Luke was a letter written to Theophilus, who most scholars believe was a Gentile (non-Jewish). This chapter includes the following three parables where Jesus taught that he came for all people—both Jewish and Gentile—in all stations of life.

- The parable of the lost sheep. Jesus connected with the poor or marginal when he spoke of lost livestock.

- The parable of the lost coin. Jesus used a silver coin, representing a day's wage, to connect with working-class people.

- The parable of the lost son. Jesus related to wealthy landowners by telling the story of the prodigal son.

All three parables reveal God the Father and his Son reaching out to people from every economic class. In each one, Jesus told the story of a person who lost something of value: a shepherd who lost a sheep, a woman who lost a coin (likely her husband's wage for a day of work), and a man who temporarily lost his son.

A WELCOME SURPRISE

Jesus told a similar story in three ways to reach the hearts of people from varying backgrounds and socio-economic status.

1. How can Jesus's example encourage you to be aware of your listener as you share the gospel?

2. Pray or journal about how you can let others know who Jesus is and that he is searching for them.

DAY 16: STEWARDSHIP

READ CHAPTER 16

"'Father,' he said, 'then I beg you to send him to my father's house because I have five brothers—to warn them so that they won't also come to this place of torment.' But Abraham said, 'They have Moses and the prophets; they should listen to them.'"

Luke 16:27-29

In this chapter, we examine stewardship (how we manage or supervise something). Jesus told a parable about two men. One was wealthy and the other was a beggar named Lazarus. Lazarus means *whom God helps*. Both men died at about the same time. Lazarus was taken to Abraham's side and the rich man went to Hades. From Hades, the rich man asked permission for Lazarus to bring a drop of water to quench his thirst. His request was denied. He then asked if Lazarus could be sent from the dead to warn his family of the truth about their eternal fate. Once again, the answer was, "No."

The wealthy man lived selfishly. He used his riches for his own pleasure. He had resources he could have invested in others or the community. He could have stewarded the resources for God's purposes. The point of the parable is to show he made no Kingdom investment; therefore, there was no heavenly dividend.

A WELCOME SURPRISE

If the rich man had invested in God's causes or in people in the name of God, his resources would have become heavenly currency.

He would have known the joy of watching his resources become God's tools to change lives. His pride and arrogance would have dissipated. He wouldn't have been flippant enough to think he could negotiate from Hell. Instead of being fearful for his family, he would have invested in their lives so they could know and see God.

Everything we have at our disposal has been given to us by God. Emotional and intellectual capacity, possessions, and talents are all resources that God gives us to manage. If we use them for the Kingdom of God, they will have eternal effect. We manage what we have for him and we give him the glory. All we steward begins and ends with him.

1. What has God given you to steward that you may still be managing as if it belongs to you?

2. Pray or journal about stewardship versus ownership.

DAY 17: THE KINGDOM WITHIN YOU

READ CHAPTER 17

"Once, on being asked by the Pharisees when the Kingdom of God would come, Jesus replied, 'The coming of the Kingdom of God is not something that can be observed, nor will people say, "Here it is," or "There it is," because the Kingdom of God is in your midst.'"

Luke 17:20-21

To better understand the term *Kingdom of God*, I replaced the phrase with the *reign of God* or the *rule of God*. It's important to remember the Jewish people lived under Roman rule. When they referred to the coming Messiah, they were looking for an overturn of the government to free them from Rome's control.

The Pharisees probably asked the question with an argumentative tone. The word *observed* (v 20) means "hostile observation." To paraphrase, "You cannot demand to see the Kingdom of God with your hostile observation." The Pharisees continually tried to outsmart and trick him to prove he was a heretic. He confronted their true motivation in his responses.

He explained that his Kingdom is not a place. He was speaking of himself when he referred to the Kingdom being in their midst. To restate his words, "I'm here. The rule and reign of God is with you because I am with you."

A WELCOME SURPRISE

The term *in your midst* means within you. Jesus communicated how we would live after his death and resurrection. The Kingdom (rule and reign) is within our hearts.

Years ago, a woman I worked with barely tolerated me talking about Jesus. Over time, she softened up and didn't cringe when she heard his name. Eventually, she began to call on his name and even give him credit when she saw his involvement in her life. I remember the first time I heard her say, "Lord," and I knew her heart had changed. The shift in her vocabulary made it clear God's rule and reign was increasing in her life. If the Kingdom is a physical place, it is located in our hearts.

In the world of monarchies, the monarchs with the most territory have the most significant power. God's Kingdom is established in every surrendered heart and expands to the territory we relinquish to his rule.

1. Which territories of your life do you need to relinquish to God's rule?

2. Pray or journal about God's Kingdom within you.

DAY 18: PRAY FOR JUSTICE

READ CHAPTER 18

"There was a judge in a certain town who didn't fear God or respect people. And a widow in that town kept coming to him, saying, 'Give me justice against my adversary.' For a while he was unwilling, but later he said to himself, 'Even though I don't fear God or respect people, yet because this widow keeps pestering me, I will give her justice, so that she doesn't wear me out by her persistent coming.'"

Luke 18:2-5

The parable of the persistent widow offers an illustration about prayer and God's justice. This widow prayed relentlessly. She experienced injustice from an adversary. We can all relate to situations that seem unyielding, such as troubled finances, broken relationships, and medical woes. This parable shows us how to respond in prayer. This woman was committed to having what was rightfully hers and made her needs known to this ungodly judge.

When Christians pray, we develop strong prayer muscles and prepare ourselves for adversity. This woman's persistence was like an army storming a barricaded city. Soldiers approach with weapons that enable them to tear down the gates, enter, and take over. We develop faith in the same manner. Commitment to prayer strengthens our faith. Christians use prayer as a tool to defeat the kingdom of darkness and usher in the Kingdom of God.

A WELCOME SURPRISE

The unjust judge didn't buckle because he was afraid of God. This woman wore him down. Injustice crumbled because of her persistent prayers.

You and I can develop a prayer life that makes Satan say, "I might as well give up because I know they won't."

1. What person or topic needs you to be more persistent in prayer?

2. Pray or journal about how you can strengthen your prayer life.

DAY 19: FROM UNWANTED TO PURSUED

READ CHAPTER 19

"But Zacchaeus stood up and said to the Lord, 'Look, Lord! Here and now, I give half of my possessions to the poor, and if I have cheated anybody out of anything, I will pay back four times the amount.' Jesus said to him, 'Today, salvation has come to this house because this man, too, is a son of Abraham. For the Son of Man came to seek and to save the lost.'"

Luke 19:8-10

The story of Zacchaeus teaches about God's character. Jesus's actions show how much attention he gives each person who is ready to invite him into their heart. Zacchaeus was a chief tax collector. He made a fortune from the additional taxes he collected and pocketed. Imagine a man wearing an expensive suit who knocks on your door. He has the authority to demand that you pull out the last five years of your tax records. You know he has the power to ruin you. You feel resentful and afraid. That's how most of the people in Jesus's time felt about men like Zacchaeus. He was not well liked.

A WELCOME SURPRISE

Romans and members of the Jewish community hated Zacchaeus. He was used to being unwanted. What did this wealthy but despised man think when Jesus called him by name and said, "I must stay at your house today"?

Jesus was saying, "I don't care what others think of you or me because I want to hang out with you." We do not know what Zacchaeus felt, but Scripture tells us he immediately changed his behaviors.

Do you know anyone who defies God? Do you wonder if they are a lost cause? Have you prayed and done things to draw them to God, but to no avail?

Let this story rekindle your hope. Just like Jesus found Zacchaeus in Jericho, he will find your loved one. He will call your loved one by name and make it clear, "I want to stay at your house."

1. Think of someone who consistently resists God.

2. Pray or journal for God to change that person's heart.

DAY 20: ANSWER WITH A QUESTION

READ CHAPTER 20

"One day as he was teaching the people in the temple and proclaiming the good news, the chief priests and the scribes, with the elders, came and said to him, 'Tell us, by what authority are you doing these things? Who is it who gave you this authority?'"

Luke 20:1-2

Jesus continued to agitate the religious leaders. He gave people hope and caused them to look to God in their troubles. He inspired them to love all people. Why did religious leaders oppose him? For one, he lived a life of humility. The leaders and teachers felt threatened by his example and became aggressive.

Jesus was a wild card. They couldn't control him or his followers. They couldn't prevent the miraculous healings or the joy and peace people found in him.

A WELCOME SURPRISE

Jesus refused to be manipulated or tricked. He responded to their question with a question.

"John's baptism—was it from heaven, or of human origin?" They discussed it among themselves and said, "If we say, 'From heaven,' He will ask, 'Why didn't you believe him?' But if we say, 'Of human origin,' all the people will stone us because they are persuaded."

Luke 20:4-6

He did not engage in debates with men who had no heart for God. He closed the door to the conversation and attended to those whose hearts were malleable and ready for the good news. His message softened hearts and made it easy to repent and express sorrow to the Father for misaligned ways of thinking or acting. People who received the message were humbled. The message of love and truth agitated the Pharisees and other prideful people who were unwilling to be taught by a nonconformist.

Could we be wild cards for the good news? What would it take for you to speak the truth and offer mercy so that unbelievers would be compelled to change?

1. Ask God to point out someone who might be ready for a change of heart. Ask God what he wants you to do.

2. Pray or journal for someone who has been resistant to the Gospel.

DAY 21: EYES ON JESUS

READ CHAPTER 21

"Be on your guard, so that your minds are not dulled from carousing, drunkenness, and worries of life, or that day will come on you unexpectedly like a trap. For it will come on all who live on the face of the whole earth. But be alert at all times, praying that you may have strength to escape all these things that are going to take place and to stand before the Son of Man."

Luke 21:34-36

This chapter covers serious topics, such as greed, power, and persecution. Before speaking these words, Jesus clarified there would be wars and natural disasters. He warned his followers that they would experience persecution. Some of his followers would be betrayed by their families.

In the above verses, Jesus puts the sins of carousing and drunkenness in the same category as worry. Drunkenness is an external practice and worry is an internal practice, but they are both distractions that take our eyes off Jesus.

A WELCOME SURPRISE

The term *are not dulled* means to weigh down, depress, or to burden. We are susceptible to being downcast when we take our eyes off Him.

If we fail to fix our eyes on Jesus, we can expect to experience some, or all, of the following:

- preoccupation with pleasing people
- worrying about money and having enough resources
- shame—the pervasive feeling that you're not good enough

- getting even with someone who has hurt you
- distracted by entertainment

God gave us a pattern for living and keeping him first:

Love the Lord your God with all your heart, with all your soul, and with all your strength. These words that I am giving you today are to be in your heart. Repeat them to your children. Talk about them when you sit in your house and when you walk along the road, when you lie down and when you get up. Bind them as a sign on your hand and let them be a symbol on your forehead. Write them on the doorposts of your house and on your city gates.

Deuteronomy 6:5-9

1. Name areas of your life where you have developed habits that reflect your commitment to God.

2. Pray and journal about areas of your life where you need to refocus on the eternal.

DAY 22: PASSOVER SYMBOLS

READ CHAPTER 22

"And he took bread, and when he had given thanks, he broke it and gave it to them, saying, 'This is my body, which is given for you. Do this in remembrance of me. This cup is the new covenant in my blood, which is poured out for you.'"

Luke 22:19-20b

Passover is a Jewish feast celebrating Israel's deliverance from a 400-year enslavement in Egypt. Old Testament law required everyone to celebrate in Jerusalem. Historians say there were typically 20,000 inhabitants in Jerusalem and numbers rose to 150,000 during Passover. Jerusalem would have been packed with people ready to celebrate. Jesus observed Passover with his disciples. Today, we refer to this meal as the Last Supper.

The Passover meal is called a seder, eaten on the first night of Passover. It includes wine and foods that symbolize characteristics of enslavement. Each food also represents Jesus in some way.

A WELCOME SURPRISE

Here are some foods, what they symbolize, and how we find those elements in Jesus himself:

FOOD	OLD TESTAMENT	JESUS'S FULFILLMENT
A lamb shank (bone)	Each family sacrificed a lamb the night before the exodus.	Jesus is the lamb of God, the ultimate sacrifice.
Bitter herbs	The herbs represent the bitterness they endured in slavery	Jesus refuses bitterness and offers forgiveness.

FOOD	OLD TESTAMENT	JESUS'S FULFILLMENT
Green vegetable, usually parsley	This is a representation of the new start and hope they experienced as they left Egypt.	Jesus offers new life in him.
Unleavened bread	The Israelites left Egypt hastily and did not have time for the bread to rise.	Leaven also represents sin, and Jesus had no sin.

Jesus broke the bread according to tradition and prayed the required prayers when he took the wine. The young men sitting around him didn't understand his words, but he established a new covenant when he said, "This is my body, and this is my blood."

Families celebrated the Passover rituals all over the city of Jerusalem. They were unaware while they ate lamb at their Passover meal, the Lamb of God (Jesus) sat at a table doing the same thing.

Jesus's birth was the beginning of a life of sacrifice and surrender for sins he didn't commit.

1. How will this impact the way you celebrate Christmas?

2. Pray or journal about what you can do this Christmas season to live sacrificially.

DAY 23: THE GIFT OF SALVATION

READ CHAPTER 23

"But the other criminal rebuked him. 'Don't you fear God,' he said, 'since you are under the same sentence? We are punished justly, for we are getting what our deeds deserve. But this man has done nothing wrong.' Then he said, 'Jesus, remember me when you come into your Kingdom.' Jesus answered him, 'Truly I tell you, today you will be with me in paradise.'"

Luke 23:40-43

Three men were crucified. Two were guilty and one was innocent. They were strangers. Each endured his own pain, but they suffered together.

A WELCOME SURPRISE

The criminals could have been executed on any other day, but their death date was divinely orchestrated. They would die alongside Jesus and he would offer them salvation.

We don't know the details of their lives. When did they break the law for the first time? What were the circumstances? Were they lifelong criminals? Whatever their stories were, the pain and shame of crucifixion brought them face-to-face with Jesus.

Every bad choice they made led them to this public execution. Humankind judged them, and they lost the right to live among their families and communities. They were stripped of all choices—except for one.

As they hung on crosses next to each other, one criminal saw the difference between himself and Jesus. He was aware he was getting what he deserved. His pride was gone. His fight was over and his eyes opened to recognize the Messiah.

During his life, when the criminal made repeated choices to turn away from God, God never turned away from him. God pursued him all the way to the cross where he made the last choice left to him. He chose honesty and humility. He turned to God, instead of away from him, and he was welcomed into eternity.

1. Who do you know that continues to run from God?

2. Pray or journal about that person. Ask God to show you how to pray for them.

DAY 24: BREAD OF LIFE

READ CHAPTER 24

"When he was at the table with them, he took bread, gave thanks, broke it, and began to give it to them. Then their eyes were opened and they recognized him, and he disappeared from their sight. They asked each other, 'Were not our hearts burning within us while he talked with us on the road and opened the Scriptures to us?'"

Luke 24:30-32

The final chapter of Luke covers a forty-day period, from his resurrection to his ascension. The chapter begins on Easter, three days after the crucifixion.

Two followers of Christ (one named Cleopas) walked to Emmaus, a town about seven miles from Jerusalem. A third man joined them and their discussion. Cleopas and his companion explained to the traveler the terrible things that happened to Jesus of Nazareth and how they had hoped he was the Messiah. They shared their bewilderment because of the empty tomb. After the long walk, they all sat down for a meal. As the third traveler broke the bread and served them, their eyes were opened to his identity. It was Jesus. The resurrected Christ didn't thunder or enter with a light show. He modeled humility. They were dusty travelers, discouraged, and processing the gruesome crucifixion. What opened their eyes? The prayer? His voice? Did they glimpse nail marks on his hands? At the very moment they recognized him, he disappeared. What is the lesson here?

A WELCOME SURPRISE

Breaking bread points to fellowship. Jesus is the bread of life, our sustenance, and he wants to share himself with us. He said,

"I am the living bread that came down from heaven. If anyone eats of this bread, he will live forever. And the bread that I will give for the life of the world is my flesh"
John 6:51

He wants to reveal things to us like he did with these two men.

He is ready to show himself:
- when we travel
- when we struggle to understand life
- when we hurt
- when we eat or when we feel hungry

1. When are you most likely to forget Jesus's presence?

2. Pray and journal about what you can do to experience more of his presence.

APPENDIX I

THE EXCHANGE

"You will make known to me the path of life; in your presence is fullness of life."

Psalm 16:11a

Experiencing overwhelm is a part of life that can't be avoided. The world is full of people and experiences that trigger us. How we manage the overwhelm is within our control. The Bible says, "Draw near to God and he will draw near to you" (James 4:8).

One way to draw near to God is through journaling. We can share our hurts, confusion, and mistakes with Him. We can expect Him to exchange our burdens for something that gives us joy and peace.

The purpose of this process is to help facilitate intimate encounters with God where you experience relief for your burdens.

THE PROCESS

Each interaction begins on a page with the Bible verse, a cross, and boulders. The Bible verse gives you permission to use the blank space and tell God how you feel about a particular thing that is bothering you. Perhaps you've just argued with someone, were recently overlooked for a promotion, or maybe you just feel lonely. Be totally honest. You don't need to be polite or afraid you'll hurt God's feelings.

When you have poured out your complaint to the Lord, ask the Holy Spirit to reveal the burdens you're carrying. Here is a list of burdens that steal our peace and joy.

anger	jealousy	resentment	guilt	unworthiness
loneliness	rejection	abandonment	control	pride
confusion	shame	unbelief	fear	performance
disappointment	regret	anxiety	bitterness	rebellion

Label the boulders at the foot of the cross with one to three burdens you identified from the table.

REPENT

Repentance is an important part of experiencing freedom. To maintain a healthy soul, we must be accountable for our thoughts, words, and actions. The burdens we carry frequently represent lies the enemy has told us. For example, if I feel jealous, I believe, "There isn't enough love for me." Or, if I'm feeling overwhelmed, I believe the enemy when he says, "You'll have to do it all because no one cares about you." I repent for believing the enemy's lies and I'm relieved of the burden. Express your sorrow in the box titled, *I repent*.

FORGIVE

Forgiveness is a gift we give ourselves. When we forgive the people who hurt us, we are released from the negative emotional attachment we have with them. Write the names of people you need to forgive connected to this particular issue in the box titled, *I forgive*. Don't forget to forgive yourself.

RECEIVE

Jesus exchanged his life for ours. We received the opportunity to spend eternity with him in exchange for our sins. Ask God what he wants you to have in exchange for your burdens. You may see an image of something. You might hear a song or a Bible verse. Use words and images to show what God is giving you in the box titled, *I receive*.

INTENTION

What will you do with the gift you've received in the Exchange? You may have a new commitment or renewed peace or joy you want to hold on to. Write your commitment to God and yourself in, *My intention box*.

PROGRESS

Keep track of changes in your thoughts, words, and actions. You might need to break an old habit and sense the Holy Spirit nudge you along those lines. Record that as a WIN in the section, *Changes in my week*.

I pour out my complaint before him; I reveal
my trouble to him.

Psalm 142:2

I REPENT

I FORGIVE

I RECEIVE

MY INTENTION

CHANGES IN MY WEEK

I pour out my complaint before him; I reveal my trouble to him.

Psalm 142:2

I REPENT

I FORGIVE

I RECEIVE

MY INTENTION

CHANGES IN MY WEEK

APPENDIX II

THE LORD'S PRAYER

Our Father who art in Heaven, hallowed be thy name. Honor God when you begin to pray. His name is holy. It's not a vending machine where you put in currency and select what you want. Experience his presence by declaring who he is.

Thy Kingdom come, thy will be done, on Earth as it is in Heaven. Jesus taught that the focus of prayer was God's will, not self-will. We pray God's will onto earth through prayer and by our actions. In another part of the New Testament, Jesus teaches about personal petition. "I tell you that if two of you on earth agree about anything they ask for, it will be done for them by my Father in heaven" (Matthew 18:19).

Give us this day our daily bread. God is the source of all we have and need. Our daily bread is the physical and spiritual food we need. We require both kinds of food to be healthy.

Forgive us this day as we forgive our trespassers. Forgiveness and repentance are a regular part of prayer. These practices clear our souls to receive revelation and direction from God, and so that we can follow his Spirit. The more they are practiced, the more the drain pipes remain open. The absence of either is like having something large stuck in the pipe that prevents dirty water from escaping.

Lead us not into temptation but deliver us from evil. This sentence describes the perfect posture for prayer. As disciples, we cannot be good or do right out of our own strength. A holy life is attained through worship and humility. God's strength is visible through our weakness.

APPENDIX III

MY TESTIMONY

In the summer of 1972, someone told me that having a relationship with Jesus encompassed much more than just going to church once a week. I was only sixteen, but I was keenly aware that I was broken, even though I didn't talk about it. The idea of having an ongoing relationship with someone who could heal those broken pieces was an offer I couldn't refuse.

A lifelong friend led me through a prayer where I said, "God, I don't want to run my own life. I want to give you my life." I began reading the Bible and worshiping (singing songs about God) throughout the day. The Word and worship impacted me, and I began to see the world differently. Unfortunately, my new life was short-lived. I lost the excitement of a relationship with Jesus and returned to prioritizing relationships with people over him.

For years I had spurts of putting Christ first in my life. I can name people God used and places where I knew God was pursuing me, but I was enthralled with my own plans which included getting an education, being married, and starting a family. I was unwilling to stop my plans to submit to his plan for me until the fall of 1983 when I started having conversations about Jesus with a fellow educator.

Until then, I had lived with the pervasive fear of rejection and abandonment. I was successful in covering all that thanks to my extroverted personality. In October of 1983, I surrendered. I stopped running from him. I turned my life around and ran towards him. I experienced immediate relief from the emotional pain that I had carried and hidden my whole life and began the journey of allowing him to have his way in me.

I was finally ready to exchange my inner chaos for the peace that a relationship with Christ could bring. The peace I saw in my co-worker drew me to her like a magnet. She had a perpetual smile and genuine kindness. When I was around her, I knew she had something I needed and wanted. The peace of Christ within her undeniably changed the work environment. She didn't wear a Jesus pin or keep a Bible on her desk as an outward sign she was a Christian. She didn't need to. Her relationship with Christ was like an unsolicited calling card. What she had was what my broken soul needed. She was authentically distinct from anyone else I had ever worked with. The peace that surrounded her broke my prideful attitude of "I'm good just like I am."

I have now lived more years in a love affair with Jesus than years I lived away from him. I'm still learning and growing, but I have perpetual peace and joy. A life with him is a stable life, full of adventure, and learning.

JOURNALING PAGES

JOURNALING PAGES

JOURNALING PAGES

JOURNALING PAGES

JOURNALING PAGES

JOURNALING PAGES

Made in the USA
Las Vegas, NV
10 November 2023

80545716R00056